NAME

ADDRESS

contents

PAGE NUMBER	SUBJECT

clarksonpotter.com

CLARKSON POTTER is a trademark and POTTER
with colophon is a registered trademark of
Penguin Random House LLC.

ISBN 978-0-593-13938-7

Design by Marysarah Quinn

PRINTED IN KOREA